# Hiring
# Humans

# Hiring Humans

## Attract, Convert, and Retain
## Top Talent in the Age of Automation

**Craig Fisher**

**Southlake, Texas**

Published by TalentNet LLC
401 N. Carroll Ave., Suite 202, Southlake, Texas 76092
TalentNetMedia.com
craig@talentnetlive.com

TalentNet LLC books are available at special discounts for bulk purchase for sales promotions, premiums, fundraising, and educational needs. Special books or book excerpts also can be created to fit specific needs. For details and permission requests, write to the email address above.

Neither the publisher nor author is engaged in rendering professional advice or services to the individual reader. The ideas, procedures, and suggestions contained in this book should not be used as a substitute for the advice of competent legal counsel from an attorney admitted or authorized to practice in your jurisdiction. Neither the author nor the publisher shall be liable or responsible for any loss or damage allegedly arising from any information or suggestion in this book.

ISBN 979-8-9889354-0-7 (hardback)
ISBN 979-8-9889354-1-4 (paperback)
ISBN 979-8-9889354-2-1 (eBook)

*Printed in the United States of America*

—

Copyediting by James Gallagher
Cover art & illustrations by Craig Fisher
Proofreading by Adeline Hull
Content development, book design & publishing by Kory Kirby
SET IN MINION PRO

**This book is dedicated to you:**
*The revolutionaries who have embarked on this journey of talent attraction. Your courage, determination, and unwavering belief in the power of human potential have laid the foundation for a new era.*

*May this book empower you to challenge the norms, redefine the boundaries, and unleash the full potential of talent attraction. Embrace the unknown and seize the opportunities that lie ahead. May your journey be filled with remarkable achievements and extraordinary outcomes.*

**Also, to my wife and three boys:**
*Thank you for putting up with me talking about writing all this down for so many years.*

*What I had not realized is that extremely short exposures to a relatively simple computer program could induce powerful delusional thinking in quite normal people.*

—JOSEPH WEIZENBAUM

# Contents

# Author's Note

Throughout my career, I've had the privilege of collaborating with remarkable teams and brands on groundbreaking projects. In this book, I'll share with you some of the innovative solutions and challenges we've conquered together. My intention is not to hand you a ready-made blueprint but to inspire you to think unconventionally as you pursue seamless hiring within your organization. At the core of my philosophy lie empathy for the candidate experience and kindness in the recruiting process.

I'm also a technology nerd. You'll see references and guides to tools and automation. But tools don't operate themselves. And companies are composed of people. So we shouldn't attempt to automate our way out of the people business.

By adopting this mindset, you can cultivate an environment that fosters innovation, attracts exceptional talent, and champions candidate-centric recruitment strategies. Together, let's explore the limitless possibilities that await when we dare to think outside the box and treat job candidates with the kindness and empathy they deserve.

We are, after all, hiring humans, aren't we?

# Introduction

**O**tsaliheliga.
(oh-jah-LEE-hay-lee-gah) is a Cherokee word that means "thank you" or "I am grateful."

The word is often used in the Cherokee language to express gratitude for blessings, both big and small. It can be used to thank someone for a gift, to express appreciation for a kind act, or simply to acknowledge the beauty of nature.

The Cherokee syllabary, which was invented by Sequoyah in the early 1800s, makes it possible to write the Cherokee language using the English alphabet. This has helped to preserve the Cherokee language, which was once in danger of extinction.

In this 1974 family photo in Tulsa, Oklahoma, I am surrounded by my parents, sister, dog, cat, and gerbil. This photo reminds me that, even as time (and fashion) marches on, things like gratitude for each other should persist. My family is large. Our sprawling family reunions (Camp Fisher) have unfolded for generations near Sequoyah's historic 1829 cabin in Eastern Oklahoma, where my great-aunt founded the Sequoyah County Historical Society. In spite of our modest circumstances in the 70's, my parents' ingenuity and resourcefulness endowed us with a life that felt abundant.

I was taught that every individual you encounter is unique and significant. These principles have guided me throughout my professional journey. Talent attraction transcends merely matching the right people to the right jobs—it's about helping them discover their place in the world and unlocking their innate potential. Conventional paths aren't for everyone. Be audacious and think beyond the norm. I've been fortunate to assist some of the globe's most iconic brands in implementing innovative talent-attraction strategies and broadening the definition of the perfect fit.

This book unveils a collection of those inspiring examples to expand your horizons and reimagine what's possible. In an age of automation, maintaining a human touch is important when attracting extraordinary humans to be part of your career community.

*Otsaliheliga.*

## Job Seekers' Shoes

Several years ago, while employed at a Fortune 500 tech company, I spearheaded an initiative to revolutionize the way the company interacted with job applicants. The company discovered that over 70 percent of its applicants never received a review, let alone any correspondence. We decided to change this by coaching two recruiting coordinators to personally review each application and provide a tailored response to candidates who hadn't been chosen to proceed through the selection process.

A few weeks into the initiative, a candidate contacted me on LinkedIn and expressed his gratitude for finally receiving a response after applying to our company for two years. He appreciated the personalized message, which informed him that he wasn't the right fit for the position but encouraged him to join our talent community for future opportunities.

Intrigued by his experience, I invited him to meet with me to discuss his feedback. As it turned out, he had been applying to the wrong department, and there were roles within the company that perfectly matched his skills and background. A few weeks later, he joined our team.

## The Rise of AI

In 2017, my team from Allegis Group embarked on an exciting journey with DXC Technology, pioneering the integration of an enterprise-level recruiting chatbot on its careers website. It was an ambitious endeavor, aimed at revolutionizing the candidate experience. To ensure its success, I surveyed hundreds of job seekers, seeking their insights on interacting with a bot for up-front queries, assessments, and interview scheduling. Surprisingly, most respondents expressed their openness to this concept.

However, those early recruiting chatbots lacked the vast knowledge base we have today. Invariably, most job seekers' immediate response was, "I want to speak to a recruiter." Needing to swiftly adapt, we introduced a link that would notify a human counterpart to connect with candidates who craved that vital human touch. Fast-forward to the present. Careers and recruiting automation have become pervasive in the HR tech landscape. AI and chatbots now reign supreme, with ChatGPT leading the way and fundamentally transforming the way we craft our messaging to job candidates. Yet, amid this technological revolution, we mustn't forget an inherent truth: people want to work with people. The empathetic connection that recruiting and talent professionals, hiring managers, and company employees provide should never be relegated solely to automation and AI. As my dear friend Gerry Crispin astutely remarks, "Someone still has to wind the clocks."

Embracing the marvels of automation and AI is essential, but let's always remember the essence of human connection, for that is where true magic lies. The delicate balance between cutting-edge technology and the warmth of personal interaction can unlock unparalleled success in the realm of recruiting and talent acquisition.

As employers, it can be challenging to put ourselves in the shoes of every job candidate. But if we strive to treat applicants as our most valued customers (or biggest fans), we can ground our recruitment process in kindness and empathy. By embracing this mindset, we can foster meaningful connections with candidates and unlock the hidden potential within our talent pool.

## Talent Tech Tools

At the end of this book, "Appendix: You're a Hack(er)" includes a "Cool Tools Link" of tools and tech gadgets. The *Talent Acquisition Ecosystem Report* from Talent Tech Labs regularly publishes the displayed graphic, with an even more exhaustive list of tools and tech gadgets. This graphic (January 2023) shows numerous tools that use AI. Given the rise in use and significance of AI in talent acquisition and talent management, recent legislation has been proposed to audit these tools for any bias they could perpetuate in the hiring process.[1] As we grow into the age of AI, remember to use these tools with empathy for the human experience.

---

1  "TALENT TECH LABS RELEASES TRENDS REPORT ON IMPACT OF AI RESTRICTIONS ON HR TECHNOLOGY." Talent Tech Labs, Accessed August 12, 2023. https://talenttechlabs.com/blog/trends-report-ai-restrictions-hr/

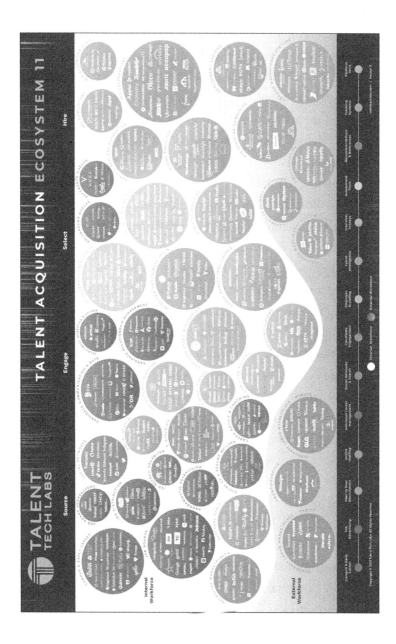

## But How Did I Get Here?

After graduating with a degree in advertising from the Gaylord College of Journalism and Mass Communication at the University of Oklahoma, I was recruited into a career in the pharmaceutical industry. The allure of a sales territory in vibrant Houston, Texas, beckoned me with promises of fortune and adventure. I never envisioned myself doing anything in the world of recruiting.

For several years, I immersed myself in the world of medical sales, hustling to establish fruitful relationships with customers in the medical field. Yet my creativity couldn't be contained. I constantly sought innovative approaches to engage with clients and make an impact. However, as the winds of change blew, legislation altered the landscape of medical-equipment businesses. And I got recruited into the growing realm of physician recruitment. Yes, in 1996, I had become a recruiter myself.

The tide soon carried me into the captivating world of technology staffing, where I found myself recruiting engineers for the most prestigious employers. Determined to hack my way to success, I taught myself the art of coding and website building. This allowed me to infiltrate the chat rooms of the very developers I was recruiting. I became a valued member of the tech community, contributing genuine questions and insights. On occasion I would discreetly share job openings, and it was during this time that I stumbled upon the power of search engine optimization (SEO). I also discovered the untapped potential of LinkedIn profiles and that keywords could be used to maximize visibility.

A revelation struck me: an inbound marketing strategy held incredible potential for employers seeking top talent. In 2007, armed with this knowledge, I launched my own search firm. My aim was to educate my clients on creating a strong online presence that showcased their company culture to prospective employees.

Leading by example, my small firm appeared larger than life in the online world, omnipresent in my customers' peripheral vision. The strategy worked like a charm, and we soon secured contracts with enterprise giants such as HP and PepsiCo.

Before long, my expertise attracted attention, and I found myself training recruiting and sales teams on my methods. Around this time, the rise of Twitter was impossible to ignore. A close friend and I seized the opportunity and initiated the first-ever hashtag chat for the recruiting community. We christened it #TNL, or TalentNet Live, and it later evolved into the popular #Talent-Net. Engaging in spirited conversations and penning insightful blog posts, I built a rapidly expanding network of like-minded recruiting enthusiasts from across the globe.

The demand intensified, and requests flooded in, urging us to transform our online weekly chat into a live, in-person event. It was a whirlwind. In 2009, at the illustrious Frito-Lay headquarters of PepsiCo in Plano, Texas, we hosted the inaugural TalentNet Live conference. Expecting a modest turnout of enthusiastic Twitter followers craving an off-line (IRL) connection, we were astounded by hundreds thirsting for knowledge on sourcing techniques and on optimizing social media. It was a moment of triumph.

My esteemed friend Bill Boorman flew all the way from London to grace us with his first American speaking engagement, serving as our awe-inspiring closing keynote. The impact was profound. Since then, we have continued hosting at least two TalentNet events every year, captivating audiences with our unrivaled content and groundbreaking strategies. The overwhelming success allowed me to establish TalentNet Media, an advisory firm built to assist employers.

The journey has been exhilarating, filled with unexpected twists and turns. Yet, through it all, my passion for pushing boundaries and uncovering new possibilities has remained unwavering. Join me on this thrilling adventure as we redefine the future of talent acquisition together.

## What You'll Learn

Similar to the contents, here are the key takeaways:

1. **Know Thyself.** Conduct a candidate experience audit to identify areas for improvement in your recruitment process. A better candidate experience leads to improved conversion rates and ultimately saves on time and budget.
2. **Know your audience.** Create diverse candidate personas with empathy. Who are you trying to attract? What do they care about? What motivates them? The more you know about your audience, the better you can tailor your messaging to them.
3. **Develop a strong employee value proposition (EVP).** This is the unique set of benefits and culture that your organization offers employees. Your EVP should be compelling and differentiate your organization from others.
4. **Determine your messaging and channels.** Once you know your audience and EVP, you need to figure out how to communicate your message. This includes the channels you'll use (social media, email, etc.) and the messaging you'll use in each channel.
5. **Build your content strategy.** Your content strategy should align with your messaging and channels. It should include a mix of employee stories, job postings, and other content that will attract and engage your target audience. Use the 5:1 give-to-ask content ratio.
6. **Build your online presence.** Develop a strong online

presence on social media, job boards, and other relevant platforms. Create content that engages your target audience and showcases your employer brand.

7. **Leverage employee advocacy.** Encourage employees to use social media and other channels to share positive experiences and stories about working at your organization.

8. **Engage with candidates.** Create a positive candidate experience by engaging with candidates throughout the recruitment process. Provide timely and transparent communication, and deliver on your employer brand promises.

9. **Embrace the Art of Job Descriptions.** Craft effective and unbiased job descriptions.

10. **Measure and optimize**. Track your progress and measure the effectiveness of your recruitment marketing efforts. Use analytics to determine what's working and what's not, and make adjustments accordingly.

# CHAPTER 1

# Know Thyself

**R**oss Dress for Less faced several challenges after it decided to streamline its warehouse hiring process. The company was using too many staffing agencies, and this led to high costs and suboptimal results. Its biggest problem lay with a warehouse in Carlisle, Pennsylvania, a small town with a population of less than twenty thousand. Ross had to compete with Amazon, Walmart, and other major retailers in a landscape of ninety-six warehouses and distribution centers employing 113,000 workers. The COVID-19 pandemic exacerbated the situation with hiring problems and skyrocketing demand. The question was: How could Ross Dress for Less attract talent quickly and stand out in a crowded space?

## Step 1: Boost Your Visibility

In a saturated market, it's essential to evaluate your digital footprint and overall visibility to potential candidates. Do people know about your company? Can they find your job listings when they search online? To answer these questions, put yourself in the shoes of a job seeker and search for the type of job you're advertising on platforms like Indeed and Google. Avoid searching for specific job titles; instead, use common keywords like "warehouse jobs near Harrisburg." If your job listings aren't ranking highly in search results, it's time to reevaluate your approach to keywords, SEO, and job titles.

In the Ross Dress for Less case, its job listings on Indeed, the platform most applicants from Harrisburg used, appeared to be two years old. To prevent their job listings from being buried under newer ones, Ross needed to create fresh templates for each recruitment campaign.

## Step 2: Streamline the Application Process

After ensuring that your job listings are easily discoverable, apply for the positions yourself to identify any roadblocks. Consider the following aspects:

- Does the job description make you feel interested or wanted?
- How easy and quick is it to complete the application?
- Do you receive an automated reply, and is it personalized?
- How promptly does someone contact you?
- How simple is it to schedule an interview?

By addressing these factors, you can improve the candidate experience, attract more accurate talent, and increase your conversion rate.

## Step 3: Know Your Audience

Once you've confirmed that your job listings are easily found and the application process is smooth, it's time to understand your target audience. Doing so will allow you to tailor your recruitment strategy, saving time and money while achieving better results.

## KEY TAKEAWAYS

- Ensure your job listings are easily discoverable and straightforward to apply for.
- Strive for a speedy application-and-response process.
- Create a positive candidate experience through personalized messaging.
- Identify and eliminate roadblocks in the application process.
- Use knockout questions to filter out unsuitable candidates.
- Apply on every platform and device to ensure a seamless experience.
- Leverage data to make informed decisions and persuade stakeholders.
- Cultivate strong relationships with HR information systems teams.

By following these steps and keeping your audience in mind, you can revolutionize your recruitment strategy and stand out in a crowded market.

CHAPTER 2

# Know Your Audience

**T**he first step in truly knowing and connecting with your target audience is to talk to them. For Ross Dress for Less, this meant engaging with warehouse employees and managers to understand who they were and how they found their jobs. We discovered that referrals played a significant role in their hiring, with entire neighborhoods often working together. While it's crucial to have a strong online presence, it's also essential to consider the unique characteristics of your workforce.

For example, if your employees come from diverse backgrounds and speak different languages, they might not all have Indeed profiles or LinkedIn accounts. In such cases, consider alternative channels like Facebook or even off-line advertising methods.

Ross Dress for Less decided to target workers from competitor warehouses by employing digital billboards, bus stop ads, taxicab ads, and gas pump ads in the local area. However, the most innovative idea came from thinking outside the box: purchasing new menus for a popular restaurant near their competitors' warehouses.

In exchange for the new menus, Ross Dress for Less was allowed to place an ad on the menu with a QR code that directed potential candidates to their job listings. This unconventional approach proved effective, demonstrating that not all recruitment strategies have to rely solely on digital marketing.

By understanding who your workforce is and where you can reach them, you can develop creative and targeted strategies to attract the right talent for your organization.

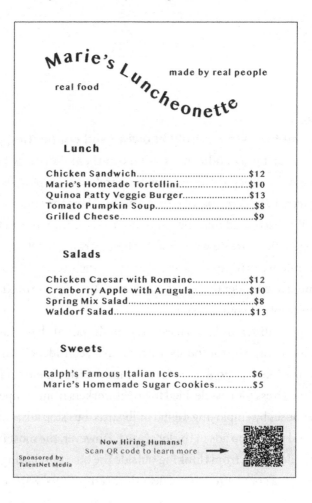

## Pet Benefits

In 2015, CA Technologies recognized that it had a reputation problem affecting its ability to hire the tech talent it needed to thrive. As a legacy software company trying to innovate into the cloud software space, it needed to rebrand and clarify its message to attract the right candidates. The first step was to identify the company's strengths.

To do this, the company conducted surveys and interviews with a diverse group of employees to get a transparent and authentic view of the company culture. One standout feature the company discovered was its unique pet benefits, which included time off for new pet socialization and for bereavement.

Embracing this finding, one HR leader suggested creating gift bags with branded pet items for employees who welcomed new pets. This evolved into a call-to-action campaign asking employees to share pictures of their pets with the branded items on social media, using the hashtag #LifeatCA. This user-generated content showcased the company's culture and generated a significant number of unpaid impressions, resulting in a high return on investment (ROI) for a relatively low-cost initiative.

The resulting value of the organic reach and traffic generated was estimated at $300,000 over the course of five months.

The key takeaway from this experience is that a company's story is best told by its people. Encouraging employees to share their experiences and celebrate the positive aspects of the company can help attract like-minded talent. Authenticity and transparency are vital, so acknowledging areas that need improvement while highlighting positive aspects can create a more believable and appealing employer brand.

By focusing on the company's strengths and engaging its employees, CA Technologies saw a turnaround in the types of technology workers it attracted, and this led to a better overall company culture and position in the industry.

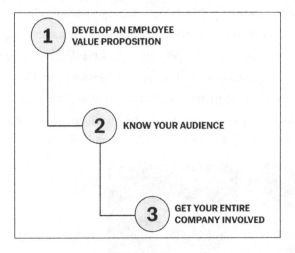

## Understanding Your Workforce
*Empathy Maps > Personas*

In 2015, while working with CA Technologies, I received an intriguing invitation from IBM to join a think tank called the IBM Futurists. This group consisted of leaders from diverse organizations and social media influencers across industries, all gathered with the ambitious goal of "hacking the future of work." Eager to participate, I headed to New York, unaware that I was about to embark on a fascinating journey of discovery.

Upon arrival at IBM's Watson building in Manhattan's East Village, I could already sense that something exceptional was about to unfold. Our group was ushered into the design thinking lab, where we were introduced to an innovative exercise known as empathy mapping.

Splitting into teams, we were instructed to create a persona representing a potential customer and draw four quadrants on a whiteboard. What followed was an eye-opening experience in which we delved deep into the thoughts, feelings, and motivations of these imagined personas, ultimately gaining invaluable insights into the customer's perspective.

This powerful exercise, set against the backdrop of IBM's cutting-edge facilities, not only sparked my creativity but also underscored the importance of empathy and understanding in the quest to shape the future of work.

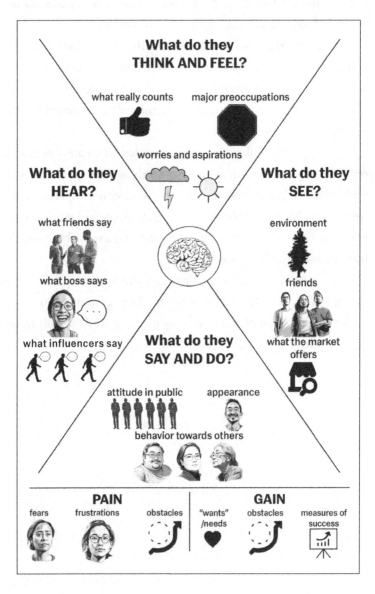

1. What do they think and feel?
2. What do they see?
3. What do they say and do?
4. What do they hear?

And then, at the bottom, what are their pain and gain points? Imagine the potential impact if you could truly understand the wants, needs, and motivations of the talent you're trying to attract to your organization. This is a concept that marketers have long embraced, but it's one that has been largely overlooked in the realm of employer branding—until now.

The empathy mapping exercise I first experienced at IBM's think tank opened my eyes to the possibilities of applying this technique to employment marketing. And so I set out to create my own version of an empathy map specifically designed for understanding potential employees and refining our approach to talent attraction.

Our recruiting team dove headfirst into this new exercise, using colored sticky notes and a whiteboard to map out the interests, influences, and needs of our target workforce. This hands-on approach allowed us to glean invaluable insights and tailor our messaging to resonate with the people we wanted to attract—just as we did with the pet benefits at CA Technologies.

To try this innovative method with your own recruiting team, project the empathy map onto a whiteboard (or draw the quadrants) and invite your team members to use sticky notes to fill in each quadrant with their insights. The process is as enlightening as it is engaging.

The success of this empathy mapping technique has led me to share my story and methodology at conferences around the globe. I am grateful to the IBM Smarter Workforce Influencer program,

PureMatter's Courtney Smith Kramer and Bryan Kramer, and design thinking coach Hendre Coetzee for the inspiration and guidance that made this possible.

Embrace empathy mapping as a tool for understanding your potential workforce and refining your talent-attraction strategy. The insights you gain will not only improve your employer brand but also help you create a more authentic connection with the people you're trying to reach.

## KEY TAKEAWAYS

- Approach challenges with a design thinking mindset and keep empathy at the forefront. By doing so, we can develop innovative solutions that resonate with the people we aim to attract.
- Survey and interview your employees to understand their attention and how they found their current job.
- Use this information to determine where to focus your hiring efforts, whether it be on job boards like Indeed or on restaurant menus.
- Continuously update and complete an empathy map to understand your audience's pains and how your organization can help them.
- Ask your employees to help you recruit more great people like them.

# CANDIDATE PERSONA

JANE DOE, PATIENT CARE TECHNICIAN
5+ years experience

## ALTERNATIVE JOB TITLES:

*Patient Care Technician, PCT*

| | |
|---|---|
| How we can target this persona | • Storytelling through ads (Facebook, Twitter, etc)<br>• Spotlight stories for the role through social media<br>• Target specialized certification programs |
| Experience, Education & certifications | • 5+ years of experience<br>• Associates and Bachelors degrees most common |
| Skills, interests & attitudes | • Service and people-oriented<br>• Management<br>• Social media |

## JOB PREFERENCES

| | |
|---|---|
| Common Pain Points | • Compensation too low<br>• Negative work environment |
| "Must Haves" in Job | • Work-life balance<br>• Competitive compensation |
| "Nice to Haves" in Job | • Guaranteed hours<br>• Tuition reimbursement |

## BEHAVIOR

| | |
|---|---|
| Goals/Motivation | • Advancement opportunities<br>• Positive work culture |
| Job Search Behavior | • Active searching<br>• Active networking |
| Where Spend Time Online & Preferred Communication/ Interview Methods | • Facebook, LinkedIn<br>• Outreach: text & email |

# CHAPTER 3

# Peripheral Vision

**I** n 2022 JCPenney understood that its career social channels had been dark for a couple of years during COVID-19 and its financial restructuring. The company realized it needed a fresh look and messaging to reboot its connection with job candidates. Taking a creative and engaging stance, the company has infused its social media presence with elements that captivate potential candidates. Here's what makes the approach interesting:

- **Visual storytelling.** JCPenney understands the power of visual content in grabbing attention and fostering an emotional connection. The company leverages eye-catching imagery, videos, and graphics to tell stories about its company culture, values, and diverse team. By showcasing the human side of the organization, the company creates an authentic and relatable brand image that resonates with candidates.
- **Behind-the-scenes glimpses.** JCPenney offers a glimpse behind the curtain, sharing behind-the-scenes content that

takes followers on a journey through its operations, events, and day-to-day activities. By providing an insider's view, the company allows potential candidates to experience the vibrant atmosphere and get a sense of what it's like to work at JCPenney. This approach adds an element of transparency and fosters a sense of connection.

- **Employee spotlights.** JCPenney puts its employees in the spotlight, celebrating their achievements and highlighting their unique stories. The company shares employee testimonials, success stories, and recognition to showcase the diverse talent within the organization. This humanizes the brand and creates a sense of pride among existing employees, while also attracting potential candidates inspired by success and growth opportunities.

- **Interactive content and contests.** JCPenney spices up its social media presence with interactive content and contests. The company creates quizzes, polls, and interactive posts that encourage audience participation and engagement. By incorporating gamification elements, the company not only entertains its followers but also drives interest and excitement about potential career opportunities. These interactive experiences make JCPenney's social media channels more dynamic and encourage candidates to take action.

- **Influencer collaborations.** JCPenney collaborates with influencers and brand ambassadors who align with its values and target audience. By partnering with individuals who have a strong social media following and influence, the company expands its reach and taps into new networks of potential candidates. These collaborations bring a fresh perspective and help position JCPenney as an attractive employer among a wider audience.

- **#Love2bJCP.** JCPenney has embraced the power of social media and employer branding by incorporating the hashtag #Love2bJCP in its talent-attraction efforts. By encouraging employees and brand advocates to use this hashtag, JCPenney is able to aggregate shared employer content across social platforms. This strategy allows the company to showcase the experiences, achievements, and positive stories of its employees, fostering a sense of pride and community within the organization. The hashtag serves as a rallying point for individuals passionate about working at JCPenney, and it creates a digital space where they can connect, engage, and share their love for the company. Through this initiative, JCPenney effectively leverages user-generated content to enhance its employer brand and attract top talent to its team.

JCPenney's social media approach to talent attraction is a symphony of creativity, authenticity, and engagement. By leveraging visual storytelling, providing behind-the-scenes glimpses, spotlighting its employees, incorporating interactive content, and collaborating with influencers, the company creates a captivating social media presence that attracts and resonates with potential candidates.

## Now It's Your Turn

Imagine relocating to a new neighborhood, eager to introduce yourself to the residents next door. But your neighbor hasn't seen you before, doesn't know your name or anything about you, and assumes you're just another unwelcome solicitor. Chances are they'll slam the door in your face or even call the authorities, all because they lack familiarity with you.

Now think of recruiting in a similar light: it thrives on pro-activity and personal connections. In an era of automation and AI, reintroducing the human touch is crucial. When targeting potential job candidates, approach them with tact and purpose.

Before emailing or calling a candidate, ask yourself: Have I made myself known to them? If they haven't encountered your organization or seen you engaging on social media, they're 75 percent less likely to respond to your outreach efforts.

To avoid being ghosted, establish a presence in their minds early on. Becoming a 3D figure—visible across platforms as a valuable contributor—increases the likelihood of forging connections and maintaining communication.

Initiate contact requests and share content that caters to their interests (know your audience). Engage with their online activity to allow your presence to slowly permeate their peripheral vision. In doing so, you'll become a trusted resource or network member even before direct outreach.

Take the time to research and engage with potential candidates. Offer value, exhibit genuine care, and maintain a human-centric approach. When they've encountered your recruiting team online at least once, candidates are 75 percent more likely to respond to your outreach, transforming cold leads into warmer prospects.

Aggregate your social content with a unifying careers hashtag specific to your company, like #TeamCVS or #Love2bJCP, so candidates can click on that and find more great content about your company's culture—and so you can track what your employees and advocates are posting about it.

The more visible you are in their periphery, the warmer your outreach becomes. So study them, interact, provide value, be human, and genuinely care.

## KEY TAKEAWAYS

- **Social Media.** Use your career social channels to feature visually captivating content, behind-the-scenes glimpses, employee spotlights, interactive experiences, and influencer collaborations.
- **Proactivity.** Approach potential candidates with tact and purpose, establishing a presence early on to avoid being overlooked or ignored.
- **Familiarity.** Make yourself known by engaging with candidates on social media, sharing valuable content, and initiating contact requests. Become a visible and trusted resource in their online networks.
- **Visibility.** Create a unifying careers hashtag and use it with all your posts. Encourage your employees to do the same.
- **Personalized Engagement.** Research and understand your audience, offering value and exhibiting genuine care in your interactions. Tailor your approach to their interests and needs.
- **Human-Centric Approach.** Maintain a human touch in your communication, demonstrating authenticity and empathy. Show that you genuinely care about their career aspirations and well-being.

- **Warm Connections.** Be present in their periphery and demonstrate your expertise and value. This will increase the likelihood of receiving a positive response to your outreach efforts.

Remember, it's not just about finding talent; it's about building meaningful connections and providing value throughout the candidate journey.

# CHAPTER 4

# Get Your People Talking to Create an Authentic and Transparent Employee Value Proposition

"**A**n employer's brand (EVP) should be built from the inside out. Just as part of an organization's marketing message should come from its customers, the employer brand should be championed by its employees. For better or worse, they are the vehicles by which the message will be conveyed on blogs and social networks."

I wrote that in March of 2009 in an article entitled "Organic Branding for Employers" for *Universum Quarterly*, the world's first periodical for employer branding. At that time we didn't have the employee advocacy software platforms to assist and encourage employees to share company culture and news stories.

Employee advocacy enables your company's people to help evangelize your brand while helping to grow their social networks and their own thought leadership. Several major software platforms make it easy to distribute great stories for them to share.

## Toyota

When it comes to attracting top talent, don't overlook the power of your current employees. Referrals are a fantastic way to bring in great people, and who better to do the referring than the people who know your company best? Existing employees can provide invaluable insight into what it's really like to work for your organization. They can share their personal experiences, talk about their job and why they love it, and create authentic, personalized stories that resonate with potential candidates.

Toyota moved its operations to a central location in Plano, Texas, and its financial services division hired a bunch of contractors to do its IT work. But after a couple of years, the company was struggling to convert these contractors to full-time employees. The contractors were content with their high hourly rates and didn't see the benefits, like using an on-site pharmacy or the company's gym, of becoming full-time employees.

That's when the company had the idea to create employee videos that showcased what's great about being an employee at Toyota. The company created an internal-to-external combined campaign that encouraged employees to share what they love about their jobs. The video platform could also convert the video to text, allowing them to update their website, job descriptions, and other marketing materials with targeted keywords.

By showcasing what it's really like to work at Toyota, the company was able to convert 90 percent of those contractors to full-time employees. The success of this video project turned into a year-long digital transformation project.

In my experience, highly produced, overly scripted employee videos don't always resonate with potential candidates. More authentic videos created by employees using their own phones can also be very effective. This approach allows for transparency and authenticity, which can be incredibly powerful in attracting top talent to your organization. Consider using a good mix of slick production videos as well as employee-generated content.

## Other Ideas to Generate Referrals

*Refer a Friend Day*

So now that we know who we're trying to reach and have great user-generated content pouring in, things are looking up. People are sharing positive stories about our organization, and we're getting noticed.

But why stop there? Why not ask our audience to help us bring more like-minded individuals into the fold? People tend to surround themselves with others similar to them, so if someone likes working with us, chances are their friends will too. That's where "Refer a Friend Day" comes in.

It's a simple ask, really. We designate the first Wednesday of every month as Refer a Friend Day and encourage our employees to refer their friends who are looking for a job. No referral fee, no strings attached. Just a nice ask and a call to action.

We didn't need a fancy system to make this work. All we did was create a landing page with a QR code for easy referrals. And, of course, we made sure to acknowledge and thank those who referred their friends. It's all about making a real connection with our audience and letting them know that we value their input and participation.

In the end, it's about understanding who you're talking to, finding a way to reach them, and then innovating with simple requests like Refer a Friend Day. When you have a strong connection with your audience, great things can happen. People are happy to share their positive experiences and encourage others to join in. It's a win-win for everyone involved.

## KEY TAKEAWAYS

- Interview your employees to understand the authentic value of your company's culture.
- Employ user-generated content to create a transparent, clear, authentic picture of your company's culture.
- Get your internal audience (your people) telling the story. That's what makes it believable.
- Make the most of employee advocacy . . . get them advocating for your company.
- Don't be overly scripted.
- Give general guidelines.
- Provide a platform that's fun and easy to use.
- Ask, don't tell.
- Make it worth their while (recognition is always appreciated).

CHAPTER 5

# The 5:1 Give-to-Ask Content Ratio

**G**ive, Give, Give, Give, Give: Ask.

Who is the front line of your company's employer brand? If the audience for an employer brand is that of prospective employees, then your recruiting team should lead the way in endorsing the company as a great place to work. Let them be the example for the rest of the organization. But give your team some direction in how to extol the virtues of working with your company.

The 5:1 give-to-ask ratio is an essential concept to keep in mind when you're looking to attract top talent to your organization. It's a fundamental principle that's based on the idea that in order to get something from someone, you have to give them something first. You can't just keep asking for favors or making requests without giving something of value in return. It's like building a bank account of goodwill with your audience or network, and you need to make sure you have enough deposits before you start making withdrawals.

This principle is especially important when it comes to

recruiting, as it's all about building relationships and trust with job candidates. You can't just post a job listing and expect people to apply, especially in today's highly competitive job market. You need to make sure you're building a relationship with your audience first, and that you're providing value to them on a consistent basis.

That's where the 5:1 give-to-ask ratio comes in. The idea is to give value to your network five times before making an ask. This means that for every five pieces of content you post or actions you take to provide value to your audience, you can make one ask, such as posting a job listing or asking for a referral. This ratio ensures that you're not just bombarding your audience with requests and that you're building trust and credibility with them.

## Pizza Hut

Pizza Hut understood this concept and implemented it through its Recruitment University program. The company knew that to attract top talent, it needed to build trust and credibility with its audience first. The company taught its recruiters to provide value to their network by posting about work on social media channels, sharing helpful tips and resources, and engaging with their audience on a regular basis.

By doing this, the company was able to build a bank of goodwill with their network, making it easier to ask for referrals and job applications when the time came. The company created a culture of giving, where everyone in the organization was encouraged to share helpful content and resources that would benefit its audience. Not only did this approach attract top talent to the organization, but it also helped to build a strong employer brand and a culture of collaboration and generosity.

So if you're looking to attract top talent to your organization, remember the 5:1 give-to-ask ratio. Make sure you're providing value to your audience on a consistent basis and building a bank of goodwill with them over time. By doing this, you'll build trust and credibility with your network and make it easier to ask for referrals and job applications when the time comes. And who knows? You might just create a culture of giving that benefits everyone involved.

Let your recruiting team be the best examples of a brand ambassador to job candidates and prospective employees through their online activity. Soon enough, corporate brand marketing will come knocking on the talent-acquisition door to engage the rest of the company, like they did at Pizza Hut.

## KEY TAKEAWAYS

- Ensure your recruiting team is the front line of your company's culture.
- Activate your team.
- Show the rest of the organization how to do it.
- Make marketing come to you.
- Build a fanatical network of friends and fans who will also share your culture with the world.
- Prioritize referrals as the best hires.
- Make it mobile friendly.
- Embrace the lessons in this article: "Mobile Recruiting: The Key to Your Next Job Could Be in Your Pocket."[2]

---

2   "Mobile Recruiting: The Key To Your Next Job Could Be In Your Pocket." NPR, Accessed August 12, 2023. https://www.npr.org/2015/12/08/458889853/mobile-recruiting-is-the-new-way-to-reach-job-seekers

# CHAPTER 6

# Improve Candidate Experience to Convert and Retain

## (The Only Metrics That Matter)

**D**aVita is a renowned healthcare company that specializes in kidney care services. With a mission to improve patients' lives and create a community of healthier individuals, DaVita has established itself as a leader in the industry. However, like any organization, DaVita faces its share of challenges when it comes to hiring top talent.

DaVita is a company committed to constant evolution and innovation in its recruiting process. DaVita has recognized the importance of staying ahead of the curve and has implemented strategies to enhance its talent-acquisition efforts.

One notable improvement DaVita has made is the integration of cutting-edge technology into its recruiting process. DaVita has embraced AI-powered tools and platforms to streamline candidate sourcing, screening, and assessment. By leveraging the power of automation and data-driven insights, DaVita can identify the most qualified candidates efficiently and effectively.

This innovation enhances a recruiting team's personal touch with candidates rather than replacing it. Over half of the #candidateexperience Awards' top-ten keys from survey results the last two years show that a little bit of communication during the recruiting process goes a long way.

Furthermore, DaVita has invested in enhancing the candidate experience throughout the recruitment journey. DaVita understands that a positive and engaging experience can make all the difference in attracting top talent. To achieve this, DaVita has introduced personalized communication, interactive online portals, and robust self-service options to empower candidates and keep them informed at every stage.

DaVita has also adopted a more proactive approach to talent sourcing and has built strategic partnerships with educational institutions, professional organizations, and industry networks to tap into a wider pool of potential candidates. By actively engaging with these communities, DaVita has expanded its reach and built strong pipelines of talent.

In addition to these efforts, DaVita has focused on fostering a diverse and inclusive workforce. The company has implemented policies and practices to attract and retain candidates from diverse backgrounds, ensuring a rich and vibrant talent pool that brings unique perspectives and experiences to the organization.

By creating a positive candidate experience, fostering a sense of personalization and care, promoting diversity and inclusion, leveraging technology, and proactively sourcing talent, DaVita increases the likelihood of converting job candidates into lasting employees who are engaged, fulfilled, and committed to the organization's mission.

## KEY TAKEAWAYS (CONVERTING)

- **Embrace technological advancements.** Employers should leverage cutting-edge tools and platforms, such as AI-powered solutions, to streamline and optimize their recruiting processes.

- **Prioritize candidate experience.** Creating a positive and engaging experience for candidates can significantly impact talent attraction and retention. Employers should invest in personalized communication, interactive portals, and self-service options to empower candidates throughout the recruitment journey.

- **Take a proactive approach to talent sourcing.** Building strategic partnerships with educational institutions, professional organizations, and industry networks expands the talent pool and creates stronger pipelines of potential candidates.

- **Foster diversity and inclusion.** Implementing policies and practices that attract and retain candidates from diverse backgrounds can lead to a more vibrant and innovative workforce. Employers should prioritize diversity and inclusion as part of their recruitment strategies.

- **Recognize the value of the human touch.** While technology plays a crucial role, the personal connection and empathy provided by recruiters, hiring managers, and employees are essential. Employers should strive to balance technology with personalization and care throughout the recruitment process.

- **Continually innovate and evolve.** Staying ahead of the curve and continuously seeking ways to enhance talent-acquisition efforts are crucial. Employers should embrace a mindset of constant evolution and innovation to adapt to changing market dynamics and candidate expectations.

## KEY TAKEAWAYS (RETAINING)

DaVita is another great example of a company that recognizes the value of showcasing its employees as a powerful strategy for talent attraction. Here's how DaVita highlights its employees:

- **Employee stories and testimonials.** DaVita leverages the stories and testimonials of employees to provide an authentic and compelling glimpse into the company culture. By sharing firsthand experiences, challenges, and successes, DaVita creates a relatable narrative that resonates with potential candidates.

- **Social media presence.** DaVita maintains an active and engaging social media presence that features employees. Through posts, photos, and videos, DaVita celebrates employee achievements, employee milestones, and the unique contributions employees make to the organization. This not only humanizes the brand but also showcases the diverse talent within the company.

- **Employee spotlights and recognition.** DaVita regularly highlights employees through channels such as internal newsletters, intranet portals, and company-wide meetings. These spotlights recognize exceptional performance, contributions, and the embodiment of DaVita's values. By publicly acknowledging and appreciating employees, DaVita creates an inclusive and supportive environment that attracts like-minded individuals.

- **Employee referral programs.** DaVita encourages

its employees to refer qualified candidates for open positions. DaVita provides incentives and rewards to employees who successfully refer candidates who are ultimately hired. This approach leverages the power of the existing workforce, as employees are often the best advocates for attracting like-minded talent.

- **Career development opportunities.** DaVita emphasizes career growth and development opportunities within the organization. By showcasing the progression paths, skill-building programs, and success stories of employees, DaVita demonstrates a commitment to fostering growth and attracting ambitious individuals who seek advancement and continual learning.

## The Key Point about Retention

When your employees become the ambassadors of your culture, sharing it openly and proudly, you become a constant presence in the peripheral vision of potential candidates. Your story becomes clearer and more precise, like a perfectly honed arrow hitting its mark. And that's when the magic happens—you attract candidates who truly understand your company's culture. How? Because you've empowered your employees to share their experiences and to give life to the vibrant tapestry that makes your organization unique.

Conversion and retention is not just about the numbers. It's about connecting on a deeper level. It's about listening to your audience, then mapping their desires and needs with the utmost empathy. It's about creating accurate personas that resonate with the core of who they are. And when you master this art, you attract and convert employees who align perfectly with your vision.

And here's the beauty of it all—when you bring in these accurate, aligned employees, they tend to stick around. They stay because the promise you made up front was a faithful reflection of what they experience within your organization. Retention becomes effortless when you've built a foundation of truth and authenticity.

Remember that all these pieces stack and build upon one another. Each element strengthens the whole, creating a powerful force that attracts, converts, and retains the finest talents. Embrace the art of conversion, wield it wisely, and watch your organization flourish.

# CHAPTER 7

# Crafting Inclusive and Effective Job Descriptions for Talent Attraction

**W**hen one of the world's largest banks recognized the need to revamp its job descriptions, it embarked on an ambitious project to create more attractive, search engine–friendly, and unbiased job postings. By developing a library of biased terms, auditing jobs, enhancing SEO, crafting appealing language, and training recruiting teams on best practices, the bank achieved extraordinary results: more than twelve hundred recruiters trained and thirteen thousand jobs transformed.

In today's cutthroat job market, a captivating job description is essential for attracting top-tier talent. But many companies unknowingly design job descriptions riddled with bias, jargon, and overall unattractiveness to potential candidates. Fear not! In this chapter we will dive into the art of optimizing job descriptions for success, drawing upon our experience working with the aforementioned banking giant.

### Step 1: Hunt Down Bias in Job Descriptions

The journey to optimizing job descriptions starts by identifying and exterminating any potential bias. Surprisingly, common terms like "drive," "his/her," and "mastery" can unintentionally project a sense of exclusivity or favoritism. To create more inclusive job descriptions, swap out these biased terms with unbiased alternatives. For instance, instead of "his/her," use gender-neutral language like "their" or "the candidate."

### Step 2: Decode Acronyms and Jargon

Acronyms and internal jargon can leave your job descriptions muddled and uninviting. To make them more accessible, replace acronyms with full terms and swap out internal jargon for clear, concise language that candidates can readily comprehend.

### Step 3: Speak Directly to Candidates

An effective job description engages candidates directly, employing "you" language to make them feel connected and valued. By addressing candidates personally, you establish a stronger bond and underscore the benefits of joining your organization.

### Step 4: Supercharge Job Titles

Job titles are pivotal in attracting candidates and enhancing the search visibility of your postings. Optimize your job titles by incorporating relevant keywords that candidates are likely to search for when seeking new roles. Targeted keywords increase the chances of your job descriptions appearing in search results, driving more qualified candidates to apply for your positions.

### Step 5: Mastering the Art of White Space

In our fast-paced world, attention spans are shorter than ever.

The last thing a potential candidate wants is to be confronted with a job description that resembles a never-ending wall of text. White space is your secret weapon to keep candidates engaged and interested.

White space, also known as "negative space," refers to the empty areas surrounding text and graphics. Not only does this powerful design element provide visual relief, but it also enhances readability and comprehension. In essence, white space is the unsung hero of effective communication.

To harness the power of white space in your job descriptions, follow these simple tips:

- **Break It Up.** Divide your text into short paragraphs, ideally no more than three to four sentences each. This makes it easier for candidates to scan and digest the information.
- **Befriend Bullets.** Use bullet points to list key responsibilities, requirements, and benefits. This not only helps break up the text but also emphasizes important details.
- **Use Subheading for the Win.** Employ subheadings to organize your content into clear, concise sections. Candidates can quickly identify the sections they're most interested in, making your job description more user-friendly.

By incorporating white space into your job descriptions, you'll create a more visually appealing and accessible experience for potential candidates. Remember, the easier it is for candidates to read and understand your job posting, the more likely they are to apply. So embrace white space and watch your talent pool flourish!

## The Transformation Journey

By applying these principles to your job descriptions, you can foster a more inviting and inclusive atmosphere for potential candidates, ultimately assembling a more diverse and skilled workforce. Start by scrutinizing your current job descriptions, pinpointing areas for improvement, and employing the strategies delineated in this chapter to optimize them for success. Now go forth and transform those antiquated job descriptions!

## Additional Examples

Creative job descriptions are a playground for employers who dare to think outside the box. These forward-thinking companies push the boundaries of traditional job postings to capture the attention of top talent. Here are a few examples of employers who stand out with their creative job descriptions:

- **Airbnb.** Airbnb is known for its unique and engaging job descriptions. The company incorporates storytelling techniques, showcasing the impact employees can have on its mission. These descriptions often feature compelling narratives and emphasize the company's core values and culture.
- **Shopify.** Shopify takes a playful approach to job descriptions, infusing them with humor and personality. The company uses catchy headlines, witty language, and creative visuals to attract candidates who resonate with a vibrant and dynamic work environment.
- **Netflix.** Netflix embraces its pop culture status in its job descriptions. The company crafts clever and attention-grabbing descriptions that reference its popular shows and movies, creating a sense of excitement and tapping into candidates' love for entertainment.

- **HubSpot.** HubSpot leverages a conversational tone in its job descriptions, making them more relatable and engaging. The company uses relatable language and incorporates personal stories to connect with candidates and highlight the company's values and inclusive culture.
- **Tesla.** Tesla's job descriptions reflect the company's innovative spirit. Tesla focuses on the mission of accelerating the world's transition to sustainable energy and emphasizes the opportunity to work on cutting-edge technology. Tesla's descriptions inspire candidates with a passion for sustainability and groundbreaking advancements.

These companies demonstrate that creativity in job descriptions can effectively communicate a company's unique culture, values, and mission while capturing the attention of top talent. Keep in mind that the specific examples may change over time, but the key takeaway is to think creatively and authentically when crafting job descriptions to attract the right candidates.

### KEY TAKEAWAYS

- Hunt down bias in job descriptions by identifying and replacing biased terms with unbiased alternatives.
- Decode acronyms and jargon to make job descriptions more accessible and understandable.
- Speak directly to candidates using "you" language to establish a stronger connection and emphasize the benefits of joining the organization.
- Supercharge job titles by incorporating relevant keywords to enhance search visibility and attract qualified candidates.

- Master the art of white space by breaking up text, using bullet points, and employing subheadings to enhance readability and engagement.
- Apply these principles to foster a more inviting and inclusive atmosphere while assembling a diverse and skilled workforce.
- Embrace creativity in job descriptions (following the example of Airbnb, Shopify, Netflix, HubSpot, and Tesla) to capture the attention of top talent and convey company culture, values, and mission.

## Job Description Template

| About you, the candidate: | Speak directly to your candidate upfront |
| --- | --- |
| What you do: | Talk to them about team dynamics and must-have requirements for the role |
| Additional tools in your toolbox may include: | Nice to have knowledge and skills presence |

- Who you are (the candidate)
  - Create an opportunity to hook the candidate with knowledge and sentiment enticing them to read further
  - Example: You love the freedom to push boundaries in the world of alternative power, to drive engineering beyond what most this is possible

- Who we are
  - Invite them to understand why your company is a unique and great place to work

# CHAPTER 8

# Branding Yourself for Success

**I**f you are in talent acquisition, recruiting, or hiring, then you are your organization's front line for job seekers. Show the rest of your organization how to be a great talent magnet and foster great relationships with the online community of potential employees and referrals that social networks offer.

## LinkedIn Personal Brand Strategy

In the early 2010s, LinkedIn approached me and my business partner, Jason Seiden, to train its salespeople on maximizing the platform's effectiveness. We wanted to equip them with the tools to present their services and company in a compelling way, using keywords in their headlines instead of just job titles. You see, those bolded sections on your LinkedIn profile are like the headlines on any web page—they catch the attention of search engines. The text itself is important, too, but those bold areas should contain keywords specific to your expertise and the kind of opportunities you want to pursue.

But we didn't stop there. We took it a step further by infusing a personal touch. In my "About" section, I share that I am a proud father of three incredible boys, and we reside by Grapevine Lake in Texas. I want people to connect with me on a personal level to get a sense of who I am beyond my professional experience.

To boost visibility even more, I strategically placed a paragraph at the bottom of my "About" section and below each previous job experience. I packed these paragraphs with keywords, locations, my name, and my company's name. This technique, known as keyword stacking, allowed me to dominate search results. When someone searches for terms like "employer brand strategy" or "LinkedIn training" AND "Dallas, Texas," my profile will appear at the top—my SEO and branding game on point.

Interestingly, LinkedIn not only approved of this strategy but embraced it as an internal best practice called "job tagging." They recognized its brilliance and asked us to teach it to all their salespeople. In fact, at the LinkedIn Talent Connect Conference, we even created the "Pimp My Profile" station. We'd dress up as car mechanics, offering fifteen-minute tune-ups for attendees' LinkedIn profiles. Executives would line up around the building to get their profiles optimized.

The bottom line is this: apply SEO principles to your LinkedIn profile. Craft a compelling story, infuse it with a touch of personalization, and strategically use keywords. By doing so, you'll enhance your personal branding and elevate your search ranking. When people are looking for professionals like you, they'll find you at the top of the results, standing out from the crowd. (You'll find more on this strategy in the "hacks" section at the end.)

## Share with the World—Establish Yourself as a Subject Matter Expert (SME) (Note for Job Seekers)

At the time of this writing, many job seekers and talent-acquisition professionals are seeing the effects of layoffs. Whether you are seeking new opportunities or just trying to attract the right audience, the following strategy will help you make better human connections.

Let's dive into a game-changing strategy for making yourself irresistible to potential employers or clients. Follow these steps, and you'll unlock a world of opportunities:

*Step 1: Create an LLC*

Establish your own limited liability company and proudly display it on your LinkedIn profile. Build a professional company page for it, adding legitimacy to your work history. This way, you'll never have a dreaded employment gap, even if you're currently between jobs. Your consulting business serves as a safety net, ready to be revisited when the time is right.

*Step 2: Select Your Top Five Target Companies*

Identify the dream companies you aspire to work with and jot them down. Dive into research on each of them, seeking insights that can genuinely enhance their operations. Write a captivating case study showcasing your expertise and how you can make a difference for them. Publish it on LinkedIn's blog space and make sure to tag your friends and colleagues. Engage with other content, comment, and be an active participant in conversations. Cultivate a human connection and encourage your network to engage with your posts. This engagement will catch the algorithm's attention and boost the visibility of your content on the news feed.

*Step 3: Connect with Key Decision-Makers*

Instead of mindlessly applying to job postings and waiting for responses, take a more proactive approach. Connect with and tag professionals on LinkedIn who hold positions relevant to your desired work. Share your research and express your interest in collaborating or gaining their insights. Remember, it's not just about asking; it's about giving. Strive to provide value and contribute regularly. Aim for a ratio of five helpful contributions for every one ask. Showcasing your expertise and genuine interest will resonate with your network and position you as a valuable contributor.

*Step 4: Leverage Your Brilliant Profile*

By implementing the strategies outlined above, your LinkedIn profile will radiate excellence. Your professional identity will be clear, and your value proposition will shine through. As people start to understand what you do and witness your valuable contributions, they'll be more inclined to connect with you.

*Step 5: Catalyze Meaningful Projects*

As you build connections and engagement, seize opportunities to collaborate on small projects or workshops. Your expertise and unique approach will capture attention, leading to more substantial projects and even full-time positions. Remember, activity begets activity, and before you know it, you'll have a thriving practice, delivering exceptional work for the companies you've always wanted to work with. This approach far surpasses the mundane act of submitting countless job applications. Recruiters might tell you to apply to three to five jobs a day, but this innovative concept propels you directly into conversations with your potential customers or employers, and it will set you apart in a refreshing and remarkable way.

*Step 6: Take the Leap*
Embrace this unconventional path to success and watch as opportunities unfold before you.

## Beyond Your Digital Presence

Personal brand is commonly mistaken as the direct equivalent of your social media and digital presence. But it goes far beyond that. Personal brand is not just about self-promotion or being visible online; it's identifying who you are as a leader, how you treat people, and how you want to be known—in and out of the office.

## Document Every Great Outcome

In the midst of your professional endeavors, be it as an employee or an entrepreneur, it's crucial to capture the brilliance that unfolds. When a good idea strikes or someone praises your work, embrace the power of documentation. Follow these steps, my friend, and watch your achievements stack up:

*Step 1: Create a Google Document*
Open up a Google document, your digital canvas to preserve the greatness that unfolds. Keep a running list of all the remarkable things you've accomplished, accompanied by their outcomes. As these instances occur, take a screenshot of the positive outcome and paste it into your document. Take a moment to jot down a few notes and capture the essence of that achievement.

*Step 2: Cherish Feedback and Recognition*
Whenever someone acknowledges your exceptional work, whether it's a colleague, a manager, or a client, capture it. Screenshot their kind words or add their name to the document so you can follow

up with them later for a quote. These snippets of appreciation serve as invaluable testimonials to showcase your capabilities.

### Step 3: Leverage Your Documentation

As time passes and the company you work for approaches your quarterly review, you can employ this comprehensive document to confidently answer the question, "What have you done for me lately?" Showcase your list of accomplishments and highlight the positive outcomes you've generated. You'll have a treasure trove of case studies to reference, substantiating your value and contributions.

### Step 4: Benefit Your Consulting Business

If you're running your own consulting venture or pursuing other endeavors, having a document filled with your achievements is a game changer. When prospective clients inquire about references or examples of your work, you won't need to scramble or create new material. You can confidently say, "Yes, indeed. I have it all right here." Your extensive record of accomplishments will impress and reassure potential clients.

Most people overlook the importance of this simple practice. By embracing the power of documentation, you'll be well prepared to showcase your excellence, whether within a company or as an independent professional. Don't let your victories fade into the background. Embrace this habit, and you'll be grateful you did when the time comes to shine a light on your achievements.

—

The quest for innovation is not simply a pursuit of excitement. It is rooted in a deep-seated purpose—to bring about positive change. Together we work diligently to refine and perfect our approaches, always striving to be better. By embracing continuous improvement, we unlock the potential to transform the landscape of hiring and contribute to a brighter future for all.

## KEY TAKEAWAYS

- Be a talent magnet and create your talent brand as your organization's frontline representative for job seekers.
- Optimize your LinkedIn profile with keywords and personal touches to enhance your personal branding and search ranking.
- Establish yourself as an SME by creating an LLC, targeting top companies, writing captivating case studies, and engaging with key decision-makers.
- Leverage your brilliant LinkedIn profile to attract connections and opportunities.
- Engage in meaningful projects and collaborations to stand out and create job opportunities.
- Employ personal branding to go beyond digital presence and show how you are known as a leader and how you treat others.
- Document your achievements and feedback to showcase your capabilities during reviews or when presenting to clients.
- Use documented accomplishments to benefit your consulting business by providing references and examples of your work.
- Embrace continuous improvement in hiring approaches to drive innovation and positive change.

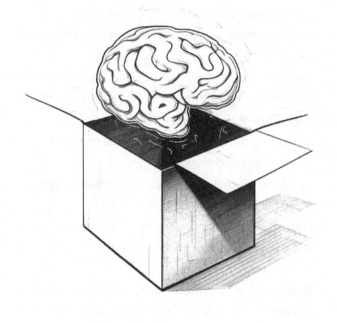

# CHAPTER 9

# Think Outside the Box—Don't Take the Status Quo for Granted

**I** n the rapidly evolving world of recruiting, it is crucial to stay ahead of the curve and find innovative ways to attract top talent. Sometimes the most effective strategies emerge from thinking outside the box and leveraging emerging technologies.

In this chapter we explore a fun approach that revolutionized my recruiting efforts and resulted in successful hires. By combining the power of Foursquare and geolocation, we tapped into a network of potential candidates in a unique and captivating manner. This chapter delves into the journey of leveraging technology to our advantage, overcoming challenges, and reaping the rewards of innovation.

## Discovering Foursquare and Its Rewards

Amid the rise of social media platforms, a mobile app called Foursquare captured my attention. Foursquare allowed users to check into various locations and earn digital rewards, creating an element of gamification that fascinated digital marketers, engineers, and creators. The app's innovative concept of earning virtual coins and competing for mayorships sparked my curiosity and ignited a drive to explore its potential for recruiting purposes.

### The Starbucks Strategy

Inspired by Foursquare's gamification and the desire to attract talented individuals from competitor companies, I devised a bold plan centered on Starbucks locations. By strategically positioning myself at a Starbucks across the street from a prominent competitor's office, I leveraged Foursquare's check-in feature and online presence to capture the attention of technology workers interested in exploring new opportunities. Through targeted online messaging and engaging content, I invited individuals to meet me at the Starbucks for an interview, presenting an enticing opportunity to escape the confines of their current workplace and embark on a new professional journey.

### Innovation in Action

The Starbucks interviews became a game changer, opening doors to dozens of conversations with talented engineers who saw the potential for growth and a change of scenery. This approach, using a platform candidates were already familiar with, not only showcased innovation but also positioned me as a nonthreatening and approachable recruiter. The combination of Foursquare's check-ins and online outreach enabled me to reach a wider audience and tap into a network of technology professionals seeking new opportunities.

### Building Trust and Authority

While the Starbucks strategy was effective, it was equally important to establish credibility and build a reputation as a valuable contributor. By actively sharing career tips, posting helpful content, and engaging with candidates through online channels, I positioned myself as an expert in the field and fostered trust among potential hires. This holistic approach not only attracted job seekers but also laid the foundation for successful engagement and meaningful conversations.

### The Outcome and Lessons Learned

The Starbucks initiative yielded significant results, leading to successful hiring for my clients and opening doors to further opportunities within the industry. This experience highlighted the power of innovation, creativity, and emerging technologies to gain a competitive edge in recruiting. By thinking outside the box and leveraging Foursquare's features, I was able to tap into a network of potential candidates and drive successful outcomes for both job seekers and employers.

### KEY TAKEAWAYS

- **Embrace emerging technologies.** Stay informed about the latest technologies and explore how they can be harnessed to enhance your recruiting efforts.
- **Think outside the box.** Break free from traditional recruitment methods and be open to unconventional approaches that capture attention and engage candidates.
- **Create engaging content.** Develop compelling online messaging and content that resonate with potential candidates and present enticing career opportunities.
- **Establish credibility and trust.** Build a reputation as a valuable contributor in your industry by sharing valuable

insights, offering career guidance, and engaging with your audience.
- **Embrace innovation as a mindset.** Continually challenge the status quo and seek out new experiences.

Amid technology advancements, it is essential to remember the value of the personal touch. While leveraging emerging tech and automation, maintaining genuine connections and fostering trust with candidates should remain at the forefront. By combining technology with a human-centric approach, recruiters can unleash the full potential of innovation and create meaningful connections that drive successful hiring outcomes.

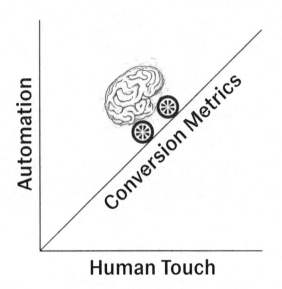

CHAPTER 10

# Prove It—The Data-Driven Mindset

**I**n the ever-changing world of talent acquisition, it's crucial to employ effective recruitment marketing strategies to attract and retain top talent. But how do you know if your efforts are paying off? This chapter dives into the importance of leveraging data to prove the ROI in recruitment marketing and talent attraction. By embracing a data-driven mindset and analyzing insights, you can optimize your strategies, make informed decisions, and achieve measurable success.

## Know Your Numbers

As a talent professional, you should always have your finger on the pulse of your organization's recruitment metrics. Understand key figures like the number of employees, open job requisitions, monthly hires, churn rate, average cost per hire, and average time to fill a role. Armed with this data, you can make informed decisions about marketing and advertising spend, ensuring you allocate resources effectively and plan for hiring surges.

## The Power of Data in Recruitment Marketing

Data is the secret sauce of modern recruitment marketing. It provides actionable insights into the effectiveness of your initiatives and helps you understand which channels, campaigns, and messaging resonate most with your target audience. With this knowledge, you can strategically allocate your resources for maximum impact. It is far easier to get budget approval to advertise on a platform you can prove drives hires.

### Leveraging Data to Measure ROI

1. **Tracking Candidate Journey.** Utilize data analytics to track and analyze the candidate journey, from initial touchpoints to hiring decisions. Uncover patterns and trends that enable you to optimize your marketing efforts and improve conversion rates.

2. **Monitoring Performance Metrics.** Dive deep into comprehensive performance metrics like time to fill, cost per hire, and candidate conversion rates. These numbers give you a clear view of your recruitment marketing ROI and empower you to refine your strategies based on data-driven decisions.

3. **Analyzing Candidate Experience.** Leverage data analytics to assess the candidate experience throughout the hiring process. Evaluate interview performance, identify pain points, and optimize communication to enhance candidate satisfaction and attract top talent.

4. **Refining Targeting and Messaging.** Let data-driven insights guide you in identifying the most effective channels, messaging, and targeting strategies. Analyze candidate preferences and responses to refine your marketing

efforts and ensure you reach the right audience with compelling messages.

5. **Identifying High-Performing Sources.** Analyzing data allows you to track the source of candidate applications and assess the quality and conversion rates of each source. This information empowers you to allocate resources effectively and invest in channels that deliver the best ROI.

## Maximizing the Benefits of Data-Driven Recruitment Marketing

1. **Continuous Improvement.** Regularly analyze data to identify areas for improvement and refine your recruitment marketing strategies. Leverage data insights to optimize messaging, channels, and the candidate experience.

2. **A/B Testing and Experimentation.** Embrace a spirit of experimentation by utilizing data for A/B testing of marketing approaches. Measure and compare outcomes to identify the most effective tactics for attracting and engaging talent.

3. **Alignment with Business Objectives.** Use data to align your recruitment marketing efforts with broader organizational goals. Understand how talent acquisition impacts the bottom line and demonstrate the value of effective recruitment strategies in driving business success.

4. **Data-Informed Decision-Making.** Let data be your guide when making decisions about budget allocation, resource allocation, and recruitment marketing strategies. Data-driven insights provide a solid foundation for decision-making, and they minimize guesswork.

In the fast-paced world of recruitment marketing and talent attraction, it's easy to get caught up in the numbers and data. While leveraging data is essential for making informed decisions and optimizing strategies, we must not forget the importance of the human touch.

Behind every data point and recruitment metric are real people with unique aspirations, talents, and stories. It is the human connection that drives engagement and attracts top talent. So as you dive into the world of data-driven recruitment marketing, remember to balance it with the human touch.

Take the time to understand your candidates, their motivations, and the things that resonate with them. Craft compelling messages that speak to their aspirations and values. Personalize your interactions and ensure that the candidate experience is exceptional at every touchpoint. The human touch adds authenticity, empathy, and a sense of connection that cannot be replaced by data alone.

By combining data-driven insights with the human touch, you create a powerful recruitment marketing strategy that stands out from the crowd. It's about using data to inform your decisions and enhance your tactics, while always remembering that talent acquisition is ultimately about building relationships and making meaningful connections.

So embrace the power of data, but never lose sight of the human element. With a data-driven mindset and a genuine human touch, you can attract, engage, and retain top talent that will drive your organization's success.

# KEY TAKEAWAYS

- Know your recruitment metrics to make informed decisions about resource allocation.
- Mine data for actionable insights for optimizing recruitment marketing efforts and measuring ROI.
- Use data to track the candidate journey, analyze performance metrics, and enhance the candidate experience.
- Refine targeting, messaging, and source allocation based on data-driven insights.
- Continually improve strategies, conduct A/B testing, align with business goals, and make data-informed decisions.
- Balance data with the human touch, personalize interactions, and create an exceptional candidate experience.
- Combine data-driven insights with meaningful connections to attract and retain top talent.

# Conclusion

**A**s you immerse yourself in the realm of talent acqui-sition, it's time to embrace the present moment and opti-mize your strategies to attract top talent. In this closing chapter, we'll explore cutting-edge techniques and actionable insights that will revolutionize your approach to talent attraction. We'll distill the key takeaways from our journey and equip you with the skills to excel in the ever-evolving talent landscape.

**We begin by embarking on a journey of self-discovery.** Conduct a candidate experience audit to identify areas for improvement in your recruitment process. By scrutinizing every touchpoint, you can forge a seamless candidate journey, bolster conversion rates, and save valuable time and resources.

**Knowing your audience is a game changer.** Craft diverse candidate personas with empathy, delving deep into their desires, aspirations, and pain points. Unearth what truly motivates them and tailor your messaging accordingly. Remember, a profound understanding of your target talent pool unlocks the power to captivate and connect with individuals who align with your vision. **Now it's time to unlock the potential of your EVP.** Craft a compelling narrative that showcases the unique benefits and culture your organization offers. Set yourself apart from the crowd, leaving candidates spellbound and eager to be part of your tribe.

**Messaging and channels are the best vehicles for conveying your magnetic EVP.** Embrace a multidimensional approach, seamlessly blending social media, email, and other innovative communication channels. Craft persuasive messages that resonate with your audience, ignite curiosity, and prompt action.

**Don't forget content strategy.** Immerse your audience in a captivating narrative that aligns seamlessly with your messaging and channels. Engaging employee stories, tantalizing job postings, and diverse content offerings enthrall your audience, keeping them hooked and yearning for more. A well-balanced 5:1 give-to-ask content ratio strikes the perfect chord, offering value while nudging candidates toward action.

Building an online presence is paramount.

**Harness the power of social media, job boards, and relevant platforms to create a digital footprint that energizes your target audience.** Craft an online ecosystem that embodies your employer brand and facilitates interactive engagement. Doing so will leave an indelible impression on potential candidates.

**Unlock the benefits of employee advocacy.** Empower your workforce to share their triumphs and tales of growth across social media and other channels. Authentic testimonials forge a deep emotional connection and serve as beacons of inspiration for like-minded individuals seeking a vibrant work culture.

**Embrace the art of candidate engagement.** Create an exceptional candidate experience through transparent and timely communication, holding true to your employer brand promises. Infuse each interaction with authenticity and integrity, fostering an emotional connection that resonates far beyond the hiring decision.

**Craft effective and unbiased job descriptions.** Employ inclusive language and emphasize core skills and qualifications that matter most. Invite a diverse pool of candidates to participate, enabling a rich tapestry of talent to thrive within your organization.

**Measure and optimize to seize the competitive edge.** Employ cutting-edge analytics to track progress, then dissect data to discern what's working and what needs fine-tuning. Agile experimentation and constant refinement will propel you forward and ensure you remain at the forefront of talent-acquisition innovation.

**As you conclude this transformative journey, remember that talent attraction is a dynamic dance between art and science.** Embrace the present moment, and adaptability will be your guiding star. Forge new paths, test unconventional approaches, and revel in the joy of attracting exceptional talent in the digital age.

**You are now equipped with the knowledge, strategies, and mindset to master talent attraction in this ever-evolving landscape.** Seize the moment, transcend boundaries, and unlock a world of limitless possibilities in your pursuit of top talent. The future is yours to shape, and your legacy awaits.

**Remember:** We're hiring humans! A little bit of communication goes a long way with job candidates. Automation can help. But, in the end, people want to work with people.

# You're a Hack(er)

**H**acks, Tools, and Shortcuts (Take a Few Things with You).

- **Try something new.** Consider showcasing your job openings in unexpected places:
  - **Eventbrite.** This delivers fantastic SEO. Create an event and title it "Home Depot is hiring warehouse associates for great jobs in Dallas, Texas" (for example). This hits the keywords that a job seeker might use to find warehouse jobs in Dallas. Paste your job description in the body of the event description. Create some free "tickets" that are actually appointment times for a job interview. Cost: FREE.

- **Your LinkedIn Headline.** This brings widespread visibility, and search engines love it. Change your LinkedIn headline (the part that's right next to your photo on your profile) to "JCPenney Is Hiring an IT Security and Compliance Engineer for Great Jobs in Dallas, Texas" (for example). Then go find and connect with IT security and compliance engineers. Your headline will do the work for you.
- **Your LinkedIn Job Title.** This notifies everyone in your network about your job opening. Change your LinkedIn job title under your experience for your current job to "JCPenney Is Hiring an IT Security and Compliance Engineer for Great Jobs in Dallas, Texas" (for example). Be sure to enable the "Notify network" setting (turn on to notify your network of key profile changes, such as new jobs and work anniversaries; updates can take up to two hours).
- **Note.** Search engines use proximity for search results. For all these alternative methods, include the word "JOBS" as well as the location and primary keywords a job seeker might use for a search, and your LinkedIn profile can come up in search results on Google. **Try this:** Open a Google incognito search and type the following into the search bar: "Employer Brand Strategy Dallas Texas LinkedIn." Then see whose LinkedIn profile magically appears on the first page of the search results.
- **Turn your LinkedIn summary into your story.** Your summary is your chance to tell your own story! Don't just use it to list your skills or the job titles you've had. Talk about what makes you a good employee, and state your career

goals. Don't be afraid to *be human.* You should have at least three things that you are comfortable sharing about yourself on social media. This is the most personal piece of your profile, so let yourself shine so prospects can get to know you a bit before deciding whether to engage.

- **Make the Most of Social Networking.** This might seem like a no-brainer. But most recruiters still don't do this right. And not much has changed since I started doing it many years ago. New platforms like Instagram and TikTok might come along, but the key principles are the same. Remember the 5:1 give-to-ask ratio when it comes to driving referrals through social posting. Here is an excerpt from an article I wrote on the subject in 2009.

—

Social recruiting is not a golden ticket to more placements. But it will allow you to build a prospect and referral network like no other medium, and to brand yourself as a professional, knowledgeable, and trustworthy expert with whom those prospects want to do business. Sure, you can make placements by recruiting from social networks. But recruiters need to be a few things before they will be successful with social recruiting. First and foremost they need to be good recruiters.

Good recruiters are proactive in building their pipelines. They don't jump straight into a new sourcing effort whenever they get a new job order. Rather, they first check their current active candidates, check with other recruiters in their organization, ask for referrals from their network, and then start sourcing new candidates as a last resort.

Our time is our most valuable asset. A few minutes a day

spent building your "social pipeline" is all it takes once you have the pieces in place. And ensuring that you are building the right network, one that is targeted to your specialty, is essential to your success. Know your skill buckets and fill them daily with new prospects by adding them to your network.

Once you have added new prospects to your network, engage, engage, and engage some more. Offer tips, answer questions, reply to posts. Don't just expect to post your job orders and have the leads come a-runnin'. You have to actively participate a little each day to build trust and rapport. On LinkedIn and Facebook, participate in group discussions and Q&A. On Twitter you must listen, contribute, reply, and retweet.

The phone is still your best tool as a recruiter. But candidate and client prospects are often more willing to schedule or take phone calls from a recruiter they have been actively networking with on social platforms. So plan to work your social pipeline for fifteen to thirty minutes in the morning, at lunch, or in the evening. Anything more than that should be done during off hours.

If you plan ahead, you will always have good material to share with your network. With social recruiting, as with all recruiting activities, you should plan for tomorrow before you leave today. Focus on the activities that will get you closer to your goals. Build your LinkedIn group and update it at least once a week. Work your Twitter network one to three times each day. Update your Facebook community weekly. Many of these tasks can be automated.

The keys to success are already in your tool belt. Your recruiting skills are the same in any medium. Your primary goal each day should be to work on the job that is closest to the money, the one with the greatest likelihood of getting an interview. Your second goal should be proactive recruiting. Keep building that pipeline for future success. Don't look at social recruiting as primarily a sourcing effort. Look at it as a method of paying your future self by assisting and conversing with those in your growing network now.

—

- **Tools for gathering knowledge about your prospects.** In addition to empathy mapping and interviewing your workforce to understand the needs of your prospective employees, use available software to help build your knowledge around their backgrounds, groups they network in online, and their interests. Here are some examples:

  - Sourcing tools that gather insights: Hiretool, SeekOut
  - Market data: Emsi, LaborIQ, TalentNeuron, Horsefly, Claro
  - Public data sources: BLS.gov
  - Even more: Be sure to check my cool tools page at talentnetmedia.com/cooltools for many more tools and tips.

# Acknowledgments
## (Collaboration)

The magic of ideas and innovation doesn't simply materialize out of thin air. This magic is the result of a collective effort and the wisdom gleaned from my network and trusted sources. Allow me to unveil the process behind the scenes and the collaborative nature that fuels progress:

- **Seek wisdom from diverse sources.** I immerse myself in a wealth of knowledge by reading books, diving into pertinent blogs, and listening attentively to the wisdom shared by remarkable individuals. These insights become building blocks for my own ideas and understanding.
- **Foster a culture of giving and community.** It's not just about taking information. It's about giving back and creating communities where ideas are shared freely. Collaboration with top experts around the world ignites a spark within me, allowing thoughts and concepts to come to life. We're all tinkering with and fine-tuning our approaches, striving to present information in the most impactful way.

- **Connect the dots.** The ideas that flow through the pages of this book are the culmination of a myriad of thoughts swirling in the recesses of my mind. Discussions with esteemed colleagues and industry experts sharpen these ideas, ensuring they are presented effectively. This process of iteration helps to prove the ROI and build compelling cases for discussion.

- **Dedicate yourself to a mission of improvement.** Our pursuit is not driven by hubris or ego. It's an insatiable desire to innovate, fueled by a genuine passion for improving the employer experience, the candidate experience, and the entire industry. This collective community I am fortunate to be a part of shares a common interest in continuous improvement. We strive to elevate hiring practices, enhance employer performance, and ultimately improve people's lives.

# About the Author

**Craig Fisher** is a renowned talent-attraction specialist, speaker, and consultant with over twenty-five years of experience in the industry. With a passion for thinking outside the box, he has earned a reputation as one of the most innovative thinkers in the field.

He led talent consulting and marketing for the largest US staffing firm, Allegis Group, and he's led corporate talent-acquisition brand marketing at the Fortune 500 level.

Craig spent much of the early 2000s building technology teams for large HR information system implementations and upgrades for customers like Accenture and KPMG. This challenge helped to evolve his approach to incorporating social media inbound marketing strategies and cutting-edge technologies, helping his clients attract top talent and stay ahead of the competition.

Today Craig is a sought-after speaker and consultant who's been featured in publications like *Forbes, The Economist,* and NPR. His expertise in HR technology and innovative approach to talent attraction have helped countless companies find and hire the best candidates for their needs, earning him respect and influence in the industry.

In 2009, Craig created the first hashtag chat on Twitter for recruiters, TalentNet Live. This quickly became a semiannual in-person conference in Texas. Skill Scout Films produced a 2019 documentary about the evolution of the TalentNet Live conference side by side with the growth of the talent-acquisition function, A Suite at the Table, to mark the event's tenth anniversary.

## KEY TAKEAWAYS

- talentnetlive.com
- fishdogs.com
- linkedin.com/in/wcraigfisher
- Twitter/Instagram: @fishdogs

## ARTICLES

- "How to Create a Recruiting Video" –
  https://recruitingdaily.com/create-compelling-recruiting-video/
- "Plug and Pray" –
  https://blog.allegisglobalsolutions.com/plug-and-pray
- "Business Lessons from the New Normal" –
  https://blog.allegisglobalsolutions.com/
  business-lessons-from-the-new-normal
- "Employer Branding and Recruitment Marketing in Crisis Mode with CVS Health's Kerry Noone" –
  https://blog.allegisglobalsolutions.com/employer-branding-and-
  recruitment-marketing-in-crisis-mode-with-cvs-healths-kerry-
  noone

- "AI and Bots for Recruiting and Hiring" –

  https://insidetalent.org/

  experts-debate-hrs-future-of-ai-and-bots/
- "ZipRecruiter, AI, and the Future of Job Boards" –

  https://insidetalent.org/

  ziprecruiter-ai-and-the-future-of-job-boards/
- "How Craig Fisher Helps Businesses Build Human Connections" –

  https://theundercoverrecruiter.com/

  craig-fisher-recruiting-rockstar/
- "Sharing Your Culture—How to Activate Your Employee Advocates" –

  https://blog.shrm.org/blog/sharing-your-culture-how-to-

  activate-your-employee-advocates
- "The Bold 3-Step Plan That'll Get You Noticed (And Maybe Hired)" –

  https://www.forbes.com/sites/dailymuse/2016/11/22/

  the-bold-3-step-plan-thatll-get-you-noticed-and-maybe-

  hired/?sh=272899ef992f
- "Elevating Your Talent Brand with Modern Recruiting Strategies" –

  https://www.peoplehum.com/blog/elevating-your-talent-brand-

  with-modern-recruiting-strategies-craig-fisher-interview
- "Importance of Mobile Recruiting—Craig Fisher Talks with @NPR" –

  https://blog.shrm.org/blog/mobile-recruiting-is-increasingly-

  important-craig-fisher-interview-on-npr